A Cow Tale

"Why Am I Different?"

Laurie Grosse

ISBN 978-0-578-52594-5 (Paperback)
ISBN 978-0-578-52596-9 (Hard Cover)
ISBN 978-0-578-52595-2 (Digital)

Copyright © 2017 by Laurie Grosse

All rights reserved. No part of this publication may be reproduced, distributed, or transmitted in any form or by any means, including photocopying, recording, or other electronic or mechanical methods without the prior written permission of the publisher.

Printed in the United States of America

Life at Cross C Ranch used to be very wonderful. But lately, there wasn't a lot of happiness to be found. As the cows roamed about the pasture, there was a feeling of discontent among the herd.

As Carly looked over at Ryrie, she couldn't help but think, *I really love her brown fur, and I don't like my spots.*

When Ryrie looked over at Carly, she thought, *I wish I had spots like she does.*

Esther was feeling sad; even her ears were feeling low. She looked at Carly, too. *I'll bet she thinks I need spots*, she thought sadly.

"What is with this Mohawk I have?" fussed Sally. "I mean, really!"

"Why, oh why, am I white? I want to be black!" complained Constance.

"I don't want to be black," grumbled Sylvia. "I want to be brown!"

"Brown. Who wants to be brown?" whined Doris. "Any color would be better than brown!"

"The cows in this pasture have it made," moaned Elle. "They are all lovely colors. Me? I am part black and part brown. This is horrible."

"Horns. I don't see anyone else around here with horns. I am unhappy about this," said Violet. "Why am I different?"

"I have a black eye! I look like I've been in a fight. I am not a violent cow!" cried Patricia in anguish. "I want to look like the rest of the cows."

The cows had a very sad day. The water didn't feel cool enough.

The playful calves didn't bring the joy and happiness they once did.

The sunshine just wasn't as comforting as it used to be.

Even the fresh spring grass didn't taste as good.

The next day was just about the same.
No one was happy.
And on and on it went. Day after day the cows complained—about everything. "Why am I different?" was on everyone's mind.

One day there was some commotion at Cross C Ranch, and everyone went running to see what was happening.

A new cow was being delivered!
All the cows gathered around to
see what she looked like.

"I can't bear to look. Maybe she doesn't like white or brown cows!"

"You can bet she won't like the freckles on my nose," said Betty.

"I can't even begin to think what she will say about me!" said Teresa.

They all stood in a circle around the new cow. And waited. And waited. And waited. No one said a word.

Finally, after what seemed like hours to everyone, the new cow spoke. "Hi, I'm Diana. You are all beautiful! And so very different! And, oh, look at you!" she said, looking straight at Carly. "I absolutely love your spots!" Then she smiled, looking at Violet. "And your horns! Those must be so handy! Just amazing." She turned toward Betty. "I think you have the most adorable speckled nose!"

"Aren't you two lovely! What gorgeous white coats you have."

Esther and Constance were shocked.

"And your hairdo!" she squealed, smiling at Sally. "However do you keep a Mohawk straight up in this humidity? It is fabulous!" She looked at Sylvia with admiration. "You have the most stunning black fur I have ever seen." Then she walked over to Doris and whispered in her ear, "I have never in all my days seen a brown coat so soft and beautiful as the one you are blessed with."

Diana trotted off to the hay feeder for a snack. All the cows just stood there. Betty was the first to speak. "Well I guess my freckles aren't all that bad." "Oh no!" chimed in all of the other cows. "We've always loved them!" "You have?" asked Betty. "Oh yes!" they all said together. Next was Sally. "Well I guess I kind of like my hairdo. Sort of stylish, don't you think?"

"Why, yes, we've always thought so!" the other cows laughed in unison.

There was a feeling of contentment that day on the ranch. The calves were playing and running about. Everyone enjoyed their youthful fun. The grass was tastier, and the sunshine felt better than it had in a long time.

The cows decided it was okay to be different. Actually, being different felt great!

From that day on, life was good at Cross C Ranch.

"I praise You because I am fearfully and wonderfully made; Your works are wonderful, I know that full well."

Psalm 139:14

About the Author

Laurie Grosse lives on a cattle ranch in Arkansas with her husband Charley. They have twelve grown children between them. Their grandchildren love their "moo-moos." They love country life and consider it a blessing and privilege to serve God in such a beautiful place.

About the Photographer

Christy Kleber lives in Northwest Arkansas with her husband Jeff. They have four grown children. They spend their free time camping and playing with their grandchildren. Christy has a special God-given gift in photography. She blesses her family and friends by taking pictures and always seems to get the "perfect shot." (She is sister to Laurie Grosse.)

www.ingramcontent.com/pod-product-compliance
Lightning Source LLC
Chambersburg PA
CBHW061750290426
44108CB00028B/2952